Ruth P. Cronly —

Heaven in My Hand

Alice Lee Humphreys

HEAVEN
IN
MY HAND

John Knox Press

RICHMOND · VIRGINIA

Two of the stories in this volume, "Ashes to Ashes" and "Libby and the Icicle," appeared originally in *Children's Religion*, published by The Pilgrim Press. The lines by W. L. Stidger are used by permission of the author and Rodeheaver-Hall-Mack, publishers of *I Saw God Wash the World* by William L. Stidger.

TO
David and Dot

In the soul of a seed
Is the hope of the sod;
In the heart of a child
Is the Kingdom of God.

        W. L. Stidger.

Contents

Heaven in My Hand

Now there came an hour at a school day's end when my Lesser Self usurped the seat of honor. And mine Higher Self sat afar off.

And the Lesser Self laid in array reasons why I should sign a contract involving shekels beyond those received for teaching.

And behold, I withstood this temptation. But the Lesser Self spake further, saying, I see within thy hands a book wherein thou writest the virtues of thy First Graders. Hast thou forgotten that this very day thou didst look to the north and behold a Small One poking peas into the ears of another; and to the south others sucking of sherbet sticks with the grating noise of buzz-saws?

And I agreed, saying, Thus have all children done in their day.

Then did the Lesser Self use the Art of Ridicule, mocking me, and saying, A schoolhouse hath ever been likened unto an Old Maids' Factory. Likewise, it is common knowledge that the Teachers who sit within do suffer with the years a deepening of furrows down the forehead. Yea, and a gradual tightening of their soft hair until it doth finally terminate at the base of the head in an unyielding bun.

And I said, These be small and inconsiderable things when one knoweth that her charges, the children, alone possess the requisites for entering the Kingdom of Heaven.

Then tried the Lesser Self one last tactic, saying, These pupils of thine are of the tender age of six. They will not remember thee nor thy gruelling services for the space of a twelve-month. Yet the moment thou art rested everything that they do shineth for thee with touching significance. Wherefore, concerning their virtues, I pray thee, be explicit.

And I replied, Then will I call to thy remembrance the little Fire-brand Ginnie, and the flower of forgiveness which blossomed in her heart. How in her ignorance she would have given unto me back-talk. And I, in greater ignorance, being young, thought that to flourish before her eyes my small measuring rod would establish discipline. And lo, as I reached in rising irritation, mine own hand struck a table's edge, hurting it mightily. And Ginnie was sore distressed. And forgetting mine harsh intentions she essayed to ease the pain by holding my offending member against her own soft cheek, saying in compassionate tones, Thy poor, poor hand! Yea, and when it was better, she rejoiced as one healed of her own hurt.

Then was my Lesser Self silenced. And it descended to a Prompter's place near mine elbow.

And I pressed mine advantage, saying, Henceforth, shall I follow Ginnie and mine other little animated signposts to the Kingdom of Heaven. And perhaps if I learn of them, then will mine own passport be paid for and ready at hand.

Now I was wearied from much argument. And as I spake the word, hand, lo, mine own did appear to grow many times its size. Moreover, my book did expand also, while across its surface ran a shining pathway. And scores of my Little Ones of divers kinds and ages did hurry along the pathway to disappear upwards in an iridescent light.

And the first lad was a six-year-old when he showed himself. But as he ran, lo, he gained in stature until he was a young soldier in uniform. And I remembered how of a surety he had given his life for his country. And seeing him thus alive and well, I cried in a hopeful voice, Billy! And he turned around and smiled and saluted before disappearing in the translucent light.

And after Billy, many others passed through mine hand with light skipping steps. Yea, I saw my Timothy turning cartwheels, and Libby carrying her huge icicle. Jeff of the Kettles shouldered his too-heavy tripod. And tiny Roberta hopped from my thumb, pausing on a beam of light to throw me a parting kiss. And finally, there passed a certain lad named Benson singing high and clear above the rest.

Then said I humbly, Heaven hath been in mine hand. And even as I spake the hand did regain its normal size. And this book lost its iridescence. But the Chronicles of the children were still imprisoned within its pages.

And I turned unto my Lesser Self a last time. And I said triumphantly, Didst thou see them and how they all remembered? Yea, and they always will. For I am theirs and they are mine: even my School Children!

INTRODUCING ROBERTA

*I*F thou camest into my room to meet our tiny Roberta, thou wouldst be apt to see her in piece-meal fashion. Mayhap a blue ribbon and a curl above a table. Or bare pink feet thrust in the aisle. Or two eyes of periwinkle blue peeping around a chair.

For Roberta is still in the chrysalis stage, having been on this earth for the space of five brief years. Sometimes when my school children of six or seven years do wrestle with phonics and the like, little Roberta sitteth dreamily with hands folded, intent on the motes dancing in the sunshine. On other days her golden head resteth on her table. Then someone bending above her whispers, Sh, she is asleep.

And always there cometh a pain into mine heart. For I know that Roberta needeth no long school hours. But rather to be lifted in a mother's arms and sung to sleep.

Now during those first days of school while she was yet ignorant of the new world which had received her, a Teacher Friend of mine did tap me upon the shoulder. Then said she unto Roberta, Little Girl, what is thy teacher's name?

And Roberta did look at me speculatively and say in all sincerity, I haven't named her yet.

LIBBY AND THE ICICLE

Now on a zero day when the world outside lay white and glistening, there blew into the schoolroom a tardy little damsel, even my Libby. Snow lay on her tousled hair, and in her reckless eyes green flecks were dancing. And, lo, at my desk she paused. And she pulled something from a sack, saying, Here is a present which I brake for thee.

Now I was several cubits away. So I saw not the gift. But I thanked her. And I chided her also, saying, Thou art late and we be waiting here for thee by the radiator.

Then did Libby stir the room like yeast. Yea, she inadvertently trod on many toes. And I saw the little ones draw aside as she sat over against them. But they also smiled great smiles of welcome. For the entire room doth rejoice in Libby.

And soon we heard sounds as it were of smashing timbers. And it was Libby tilting the chair too far backwards. And at the lunch hour she churned her chocolate milk, splashing what she termed Brownie Butter down the necks of her classmates.

Moreover, she did punish the room with sudden bursts of whistling. And for no reason save that she had heard a robin outside.

Now later on the aforesaid day, Libby opened our understanding with wondrous words she coined while reading. And suddenly I interrupted her sharply. For I had espied a huge wet spot on the festive blotting paper adorning my desk.

And Libby, as soon as she had looked, did begin to weep bitterly and to say,

Oh, mine icicle has melted! It was thy present. And it looked like curly glass. And it had a rainbow inside.

Then spake I unto her and all the other little lads and damsels, saying, Thy teacher still hath the icicle.

And they all did look. And, lo, on the red paper before them lay the marvelous contours of an icicle. Save that it was of a giant size which delighteth children. And as they gazed, they did marvel.

Now I meditated long on the matter. And I considered how such things as rainbows, stars, and icicles seem always to belong unto Libby. And how, albeit in a devastating way, she tryeth ever to divide them.

And I remembered also that I did have twenty-nine other children whose daily walk to the cloakroom is ordered aright.

They, too, do wonder over the crystalline beauty of a snowbound world. Yet they bring it not in save on their cloaks and little faces.

Yea, it taketh a Libby to leave the fairy imprint of an icicle forever on a piece of red blotting paper.

RECESS REVELATION

RAIN did beat vehemently against the schoolhouse, insomuch that there was no outdoor recess.

Within, the Little Ones formed in unregimented groups rejoicing that there was no Director to say, Thus shalt thou do at such and such a moment.

And lo, the small circle which stood over against me did forget my presence. And their tongues were loosed. And they spake of the various dinner invitations they had accepted from the Lord's House on the day previous.

And there was much boastful switching of tiny dress tails amongst my maidens. And many braggarts amongst the lads concerning new puppies and golden slabs of cake acquired at the abodes of Grandmothers.

Then, as hath been true always, one pupil brought forth the Unexpected. A tiny fay of a maiden, being too young to discern between things of the Body and those of the Spirit, saith in a soft conversational tone, I didn't see who took Jesus home.

Now such soul-searching words fell on mine ears with the impact of an atomic bomb. But the children reasoned earnestly one with another, saying, Who could have taken Him home?

And suddenly I was filled with the passionate hope that one little tongue might name me as the probable Hostess of the Great King.

Then Kathy stepped forth. Kathy, mine accurate maiden who pondereth well before speaking. And she laid her small hands in precise fashion on her hips, and she did weigh her words as carefully as a judge pronouncing sentence. And Kathy spake thus: *It would have been Old Barney.*

Now these astounding words did seem a sacrilege, and I expected instant denial. But the listeners seemed of the same mind. For they nodded their heads in agreement, saying, Yes, Old Barney it would certainly be.

Now Barney is the social outcast of the town. A Derelict of a man. But one nevertheless who, when not in his cups or roving, delighteth to make peach-kernel baskets and divers other whittled toys for children. Yea, and on occasion ministereth unto those inmates of the County Home possessed of ungrateful In-laws.

Thus, while it laid my pride in the dust to remember that of all the influential congregation, Barney had been named its most generous soul, yet dared I not distrust the spiritual discernment of children.

So, as for me and mine, Barney it must always be!

THE LADY IN RED

*T*ORNADOES have an affinity for our little city. But the one today did only flirt with us, passing by at a distance of two miles.

Yet its rumble brought to my mind the genuine twister of years ago. And I remembered Billy. For Billy and the word twister are synonymous.

Now from the first day he entered school, I dubbed him my Crown Prince of Comedy. For verily he was a mimic, and did otherwise fill his days with antics and nonsense.

Then came the spring morning when an unearthly green haze filled the universe. And great drops of vapor clung to the windows. And a swift darkness came down upon the earth.

And I said unto my Little Ones, Let us sing a song until this cloud passes us by.

Then did Billy espy on the cheek of his best friend a tear that hung and trembled. And in the next instant he was in the aisle. And he caught the fearful little one to his side. Yea, and concealing his own fear, he began to sing a hit tune, Oh, the Lady in Red. Then as houses a block away snapped from the force of the storm, Billy swayed more to the rhythm and sang louder.

Now as I sat alone in my schoolroom reviewing this memory, I felt a light touch on my shoulder. And as I turned I beheld a young Infantryman. And lo, he had also been a member of what I termed The Twister Grade. Yet twelve years had passed and now he had the atmosphere of War upon him. For on his breast were many battle stars, and on his shoulder the insignia of the famous Third Division.

And straightway he said unto me, I would tell thee of Billy. And I said, There be radii of the heart forever reaching from a teacher to her pupils. Lo, I was thinking of thee and of Billy as thou didst enter.

And the young soldier said, Billy was a Captain. Yet would I speak rather of his antics and capers on the breakthrough from Anzio to Rome.

Then said the Infantryman, On the beachhead we dreamed continuously of the day when we would drive back the Germans. Yet when the long-awaited day arrived, then did we find our bodies tense and our lips dry. For we knew that the mountains around us were ringed with enemy gun emplacements. Yea, and that the ground we must cross was an unprotected wasteland.

Then, just as the signal to advance was given, Billy came to our rescue. With a swagger which resembled naught so much as a Nazi goose-step, he started walking toward that gunfire singing the hit tune of our childhood, Oh, the Lady in Red.

And a new warmth began to flow through our veins, steadying our nerves. Yea, and we were soon singing with him. And we were out on that piece of convulsed earth racing for the mountains. However, when the shells rained down upon us with their roars and piping whistles, then would we fling ourselves downward upon the earth. But the moment an explosion ceased,

Billy would rise and yell, What a splash! Or peradventure, That's just a dud!

So ducking, yet ever pressing onward, we finally reached the foothills. And there Billy got the shell with his name on it.

Here the Infantryman paused. And I saw the pulse beating violently in his throat as it had ever done when he was overcome with emotion. But he straightened suddenly, saying, It was one great day when we looked down and saw Rome on her Seven Hills. But half of our joy was quenched in that Billy was not there to strut in and bestow kisses on the Italian Beauties.

Now I did wipe mine eyes, and I said, To hear thee speak one would think Billy a swaggering, devil-may-care Fire-Eater. But thou foolest me not. For even at the age of six years did he not put on just such a free act? And all because of the loneliness and terror of others. Yea, did not you also see him on that day of the tornado draw a terror-stricken little shape to his side?

Then did the Infantryman smile sheepishly and say, Lo, I was that timorous youngster.

And straightway the Young Infantryman and I did sit together in a companionable silence. And I gazed long upon him. And save for his uniform and medals, he might still be my six-year-old pupil.

Save for a difference in his eyes. For now they gazed far beyond the schoolroom seeing strange and terrible things which I can never understand.

But my eye-span went not beyond the windows. For I was beholding in the first aisle a lithe, graceful figure shaking slender little hips. And I heard again a clear childish treble . . . Oh, the Lady in Red!

CAT EYES

Outside the windows, robins fluttered on the telephone wires heralding the Spring. And within the schoolroom, tiny Roberta flitted also. Yea, she did weave between the aisles in endless playtime. Then suddenly she sank contentedly into her small chair and began to converse with herself.

Now, at that moment, it so happened that a silence fell upon the classroom. And Roberta could be heard crooning dreamily: I was six months old before I left Heaven-House.

This remarkable statement caused a few oh's and ah's. But none of the listeners dared to peer deeper into Roberta's wonder-world. Nevertheless, the story teller was flattered by the attention, and elaborated, saying, I was helping God put eyes into the heads of babies. If they were good children I gave them blue or brown eyes. But concerning the bad ones, God said, Give them green eyes like unto those of a cat.

Amazement now held the audience spellbound. That is, all save one Doubting Thomas. His brown eyes were glittering pinpoints of curiosity. And he pointed a small forefinger straight in my direction, saying, Behold the Teacher! Hath she not green eyes?

Now indeed did astonishment abound. And thirty souls gazed at me in bewilderment. Yea, and a few with accusation.

But Roberta hath finesse. Above the shocked silence came her serene voice saying, God maketh Teacher's eyes differently. He fashioneth them of jewels like unto those in our morning worship song.

This explanation did the listeners accept gladly. For no small child liketh to see his Teacher set at naught. Roberta, likewise, sank back satisfied. And all over the room I could hear a soft humming of When He Cometh, When He Cometh, to Make Up His Jewels.

Now, that evening I gazed long into my mirror. And, lo, for the first time in my life, mine eyes were no longer a reproach unto me. Yea, I stared long at the green flecks set in gray. And I smiled, for I remembered that of necessity they had become unto Roberta emeralds or real jade. Verily, as I continued to gaze at the greenish orbs, I found mine own self singing another line from the Jewel Song. And these were the words: They shall shine in their beauty. . . .

And almost I believed it.

THE DIFFERENCE

*P*AMELA was a Personage. As I approached the rented weather-beaten cottage, I knew that had I been her dinner guest a century before, I would be passing through gates of wrought-iron unto trellised galleries.

For Pamela stood by her mother and welcomed me with adult dignity. She wore a made-over dinner dress in my honor. And its tiny ruffled skirt swished with importance. It was after her mother had excused herself, and I dropped into an ancient Chippendale chair, that Pamela proved herself only a little damsel and six years old.

We had hoped that you would not sit there, she began politely. That chair falls if a grown-up uses it. Everything is too old, she confessed wistfully. We never speak of it to anyone, but I think it right to tell such things unto a Teacher.

Here began I a hasty denial, but it was impossible to stem the tide of Pamela's release. She was bubbling over. She pointed to a portrait in oils. Behind that gentleman, she continued primly, there is no papering at all. The rain leaked in and washed away the roses from the walls. She drew a deep sigh and I said within my heart, I must listen to such engaging frankness no longer. And I grasped at a glimpse of the damsel's mother busy with last-minute details of the dinner. Likewise, I welcomed the odor of savory stuffings as a safer topic of conversation.

Pamela, I ventured, thy mother must be a wonderful cook.

Then did the little damsel draw herself up and give me a look of delicate injury. Yet when she spake, her pride was intact. She had not lost caste.

My mother is no cook, she declared in her low clear voice: She is the Lady What Cooks!

Now I challenge the Wise Ones of Earth to make a finer distinction.

CHRISTMAS GIFT

VERYTHING was Christmas-
wise. Yea, there was a flurry of tinsel in the Second-grade
Teacher's hair. And the tree did glow and shimmer. It had gold
and silver ropes a-swing. And my wrenched backbone felt as
though it were suspended also.

Now I groaned aloud for weariness. And the Second-grade
Teacher said, Art thou really sick?

And I answered, Nay, I have only an ache and a pain plus
a hurting-all-over. Then as we laughed, we heard the patter of
small footsteps outside the door. And I whispered, Some little
Eavesdropper can't wait until the morrow. And we arose hur-
riedly and went unto our boarding house.

And the next morning the tree stood breathless with beauty.
And beneath its shining arms were many gifts for the teachers.
Moreover there was much ceremony over the acceptance of these
latter gifts.

Now in the rear of the room sat a Lad. And he had come
unto us lately from the mountains. And to me, his teacher, he
always seemed naught but an enormous pair of eloquent brown
eyes attached to a set of undernourished arms and legs. And his
blue denim Christmas suit was fearfully and wonderfully made.

And on this day he was the last one to come forward. And lo, as he approached, I could see his bright red holiday tie somersaulting over the excited little heart beneath. And he said with a breathless rush of words, I fotched you this. And the words sounded reckless and extravagant.

Then he slowly opened one grimy hand as though he handled a diamond. And there within the moist, dirty little palm lay what had lately been a chocolate-covered pill. Save that now the brown coating had melted, revealing a pellet of bilious hue.

Now I accepted this gift with solemn gratitude. But I hid it from all curious eyes. Yea, I wrapped it in Christmas paper, and hung it near the top of the tree.

And the Lad was pleased. And he said with quick, shy happiness, You don't belong to thank me. And he sidled up closer and whispered, Hit be for thy hurtin'-all-over.

Then straightway I understood whose footsteps we had heard beyond the door. And suddenly the Lad's seven small words made the pill of more value than the costly gifts bearing Merry Christmas in gold upon them. And I marvelled that so often the outward covering of a gift gave so little hint of the wealth of love and solicitude within.

Now that night I rehearsed unto the Second-grade Teacher the whole story. And I withheld not from her sight the pill. And she laughed merrily and said, Dost thou expect this strange remedy to revive thee?

And I chided her, saying, Let no one call this remembrance poor. For behold it is a Love-cure. Verily, it hath been prescribed expressly for the worst of all human ailments: A Hurtin'-All-Over.

HONOR TO WHOM HONOR

OUR school Janitor is an ancient Ethiopian and unlearned in Books. Nevertheless, he possesseth such courtesy and elemental Knowledge that my Little Ones in all innocence sometimes speak of him as the Dark Principal.

And today as he entered at the school's end, the children did flock around to learn of him. And the burden of the conversation was Names.

And I interrupted them, saying, I once taught twins whose real names were Mediterranean Sea and Pacific Ocean, albeit they were known as Med and Pacy.

At this juncture the Janitor laughed uproaringly. Then he spake unto us in his own tongue, saying, My mother had queer namin' notions, too. She called every girl baby after a flower. I had sisters named Magnolia, Petunia, Verbena, and Pansy.

Here the Ancient Man did lay his mop against the wall, adding with a new tone of respect, Yassum, all of my sisters were called by the names of flowers except Mis' Gloria.

Now, thought I, here lieth some strange African superstition or taboo. Therefore prodded I the Janitor further, saying, Mayhap thy mother named the maiden Gloria after the Morning Glory.

But the Janitor shook his head. Mis' Gloria, he did explain, were the name of my mother's young Mistis. And when the name were passed on to my baby sister, all of us chillun were called together. And our mother explanified the love she held for the name, and how unfitten it would be for us to ever uncouple the Mis' from the Gloria.

But did it not seem passing strange, interrupted I, to speak of thine own sister always as Miss?

Then answered the Janitor in gentle reproof, It seemed no beholden duty to us. We held it a pleasure to honor the name of the young Mistis.

Now the Janitor went his way with his mops and brushes. But he left me with many thoughts. And I spake unto my children, saying, I verily believe that our Janitor hath taught you a greater lesson today than any set forth by thy teacher. For lo, some of you do question Those in Authority over you, with the sole word, Huh? And others amongst you ever answer your Elders in like manner, saying, Uh-Huh. And I wish, ended I, that all of you might remember the kindly Janitor's lesson in courtesy.

Then spake one small lad on whom no mantle of graciousness hath descended. And he was truly desirous of learning the Janitor's lesson. And he questioned me earnestly, saying, Huh?

THE BASSO OF BENSON

*T*HESE experts who declare that the singing of children nearest approacheth that of the Heavenly Choir, have never heard Benson punish the air with song.

Yet at first, this lad possessed no defeatist attitude. Loudly he did mingle his deep-throated baying with the sweet, flute-like notes of his fellows. And ever and anon, with chest thrust forward and sorrel-colored cowlick upright in confidence, he would turn toward me, his teacher, for commendation.

Yea, Benson was agreeable about dispensing his discords. Since a confusing string of Do-re-mi's were expected of him, he decided loyally that they should not be lacking.

Then came the inevitable day when a sensitively attuned lad cried out at Musick Period, Benson hath carried me away from mine own notes with his low sounds of a bullfrog. And another added, Benson soundeth like unto one in a deep well.

In such manner was the enthusiasm of my fiery little Red Head curbed and his pride abased. And the fence between him and the La-ti-do's did appear so formidable that he began unconsciously to draw in his breath and stretch on tiptoe in a mighty effort to climb over into the Land of Harmony.

Now was I perplexed beyond measure. And I said within myself, Musick should be scattered abroad and gathered up in some way by every creature. This failure of Benson's must not remain forever in his recollection.

And in mine extremity I remembered how the lad, beyond all others, was able to feel the rhythm of Musick. Yea, and likewise give the interpretation thereof.

Wherefore, from that day, there began in my room a season of skipping, dancing, and galloping. And Benson, leaving all inhibitions behind, did interpret all manner of creatures from birds and fairies unto coarse-voiced tugboats and ogres.

It was during this new regime in Musick that a foreign Master Musician visited his kinsman in our city. And lo, he appeared suddenly in our midst, saying, I fain would hear the voices of young Americans singing.

And he inscribed one simple measure from a Mother Goose melody upon the board, using the high notes which were as blind spots unto Benson. And my class sang with bell-like tones of purity. And Benson, forgetting his shame, did add his distressful bass croakings.

And forthwith the Master paused, touching the curls of Linda, my choicest singer. And he saith unto her, Repeat this same measure. And Linda, with a flutter of curls and pride, sang it clearly and in tune.

Then saith the Musician, Behold an accurate damsel! She shall have this silver charm-piece because of her correct singing.

And the great Master paused a second time. Now he, being truly great, had perceived above Benson's grotesque singing, his perfect rhythmical swaying. Wherefore did the man take a record of Musick from his portfolio, and putting it on a victrola, say unto the class, Tell me, now I pray, of what this Musick speaketh.

And suddenly the air was alive with the Musick. At first there was a commanding entry, followed by the dynamic sound of hoof-beats. These swelled into a mighty thundering so great that it seemed to shake the very earth. Then the martial sounds receded, growing fainter and fainter and finally dying away in the distance.

And straightway my Little Ones began to give their interpretations of the Musick. And one damsel who lispeth saith, It wath the thound of a great wind thinging. And a cocksure lad urged, Nay, it was the noise of many machines at a carnival. Yet with all their pronouncements, none was wise enough to read the meaning of the Musick aright.

Then glanced I at Benson. And lo, by the light of his countenance I knew he had been swept forward by the thundering hoofs. And suddenly, forgetful of the assemblage, he cried out in a loud voice, saying, Horses! Hundreds of men on galloping horses! Far away at first. Then splitting mine ears. Then gone!

Now was the Musick Master truly stirred. And he laid some coins, to the amount of several shekels, in the hands of Benson, saying, This pupil hath outdistanced the others in that he hath gotten beyond the technique of Musick, and found its Soul.

And forthwith the recess bell did ring. And Benson was surrounded by a host of admirers. And for the space of fifteen minutes, he turned the coins over in his palms, communicating happily all the while with his schoolmates.

And when the gong sounded again, Benson ran for the line. And lo, he suddenly began to move in the unmistakable rhythm of the Cossack Riders who had thundered so magnificently from the Musick Master's record.

Now was I truly exalted. But as swiftly humbled. For I remembered how nearly I had allowed Derision to leave its shadow on the one pupil possessing the true passport into the Realm of Musick.

LO, THE POOR TEACHER

I HAVE somewhat against the Pilgrims. And it happened on this wise:

On the eve of one Thanksgiving, I arrayed myself in a rose-colored dress. And there were sprays of blue silk periwinkles woven throughout its length and breadth. And the cost thereof flattened my purse. Yet I soothed my conscience with the thought that often a teacher's apparel hath power to determine a child's mood for the day. And also I had a different and truer reason.

Yea, a Friend of mine was arriving that morning from a distant country. And I was far from the mood of sackcloth and ashes.

Now as I waited, the school day drew to a close. And I decided to fill the intervening minutes with the experiences of our Pilgrim Fathers. And I spake of the voyage on the Mayflower. And the privations of that first hard winter. Yea, and I accented the strange customs and sober dress of three hundred years ago.

And the stories pleased the little ones. And their tongues were loosed. And they asked many questions. Verily one small lad's hand was like unto a windshield wiper in its movements from side to side, to gain my attention.

Therefore, to ease his burden I did ask him to name the ship which had brought our Forefathers hither. And he drawled, Hard-Ship.

Now at this moment, footsteps sounded at the main entrance of the school, and I hurried to greet my Friend. And when we were come into the room again, then made I the visitor known. And immediately, my small Inquirer began to wave again for a hearing.

And I felt gay and confident. And I whispered unto my Friend, Thou art going to get a kick from this. For yonder lad always hath something of originality and meaning to impart.

And I spake aloud, and I said, What wouldst thou that I answer?

And the lad said earnestly, Wast *thou* ever a Pilgrim?

And straightway my Friend made a strange choking sound. Verily he was forced to withdraw from the room. For he was bending over with inward laughter.

And never, not even unto this day, have I asked the little Inquirer the reason for his question.

ONE USES THE GUN

*A*BOVE, the sky was a tranquil blue. But below, on the playground, there arose a thick cloud of dust. And it betokened the milling together of many agitated feet.

Peace has come to men at last, I mused, but their small sons still play the game of War. And I looked closer. And lo, in the center of the mob, I beheld a fiery-red cowlick. And it belonged to my violent new pupil, Benjamin. There he stood four-square before the multitude, his whole body a flaming ball of fury. In his small right hand he was brandishing an ancient-looking pistol. Yea, and above the teasing laughter, one could hear him affirming wildly, *I shall pull this trigger and shoot this gun.*

Now, as I argued that a hand too small to form the letter "A" could scarcely shoot a rusted gun, there was a tap upon my shoulder. And it was an high school pupil. And he whispered with terrible clarity, It's his Grandpap's and it's loaded!

In the tense moment that followed, the whole earth did seem to hang motionless in suspense. Horror-stricken, I gazed at my little ones. They still surrounded the new lad in a sort of hypnotic trance. Then tried I to speak but my voice was lost in fear. Finally, a Power beyond myself forced me to slip behind the lad and knock the gun from his hands.

As it struck the earth with a harmless thud, Benjamin likewise threw himself to the ground, clenching his fists and beating them in the dust. And he sobbed desperately, crying, *I shall yet shoot the gun.*

And the high school lad tapped upon me the second time. And he said, This kid hath just moved to our street. His daddy was a mess sergeant who was never taught to fire a gun. But when things got so hot on Okinawa, he ran out to fight and was killed trying to man a machine gun. Since then the kid hath almost gone nuts. He hath some phony idea that he must learn to shoot for his old man.

Then glanced I at Benjamin. And lo, he was wavering to his feet, and he resembled nothing so much as a deflated balloon. And I found I could hold my peace no longer. And I heard my voice as though it were the voice of a stranger saying, *Thou shalt indeed shoot this gun, yet not on a playground!*

And consternation was written on the faces of all the listeners. And I felt a third tap on my shoulder. And, lo, it was my Principal. And his face was flushed. And I expected dismissal. But he merely said, I am better versed in shooting than thou. Only mine age hath hindered me from pulling one trigger for my country. Wherefore know I the frustration in the heart of this child. And I fain would take him and give him his heart's desire.

Now the two departed immediately. And there began to burn within me a woman's desire to know all. And as the day drew on to its close, I phoned the Principal. And I said, Are the School Trustees gunning for thee yet?

{ 40

And he answered in an unexcited voice, Nay.

And I pressed him further, saying, Tell me everything.

Then said the Principal, No sooner had we reached a solitary wood than I set up a target and placed the pistol in the lad's hand. Yea, and I supported his forearm and fingers. And together we pulled the trigger. And, lo, nothing happened. Then heaved we mightily. And there followed an explosion which seemed to shatter the universe. Afterwards, we stood quietly until the wild rebellion had died from the lad's eyes. Then said I unto him, Benjamin, thy father died to bring us this peaceful world of no guns.

And he answered tremulously, I only wanted to shoot one shot for him.

Thus, continued the Principal, one bullet satisfied a child's desire to uphold the integrity of his father. And the Principal added, Many are the strange devices a teacher must use to make a heartsick lad feel at home and vindicated.

Now the words were true. For on the following morning the Principal and Benjamin chanced to enter the school building together. And Benjamin walked in happy confidence. His red cowlick waved proudly in the wind. And gazing at the reckless little face, I knew I was seeing the countenance of the young Mess Sergeant on the front lines of Okinawa.

JEFF OF THE KETTLES

F Little Ones there be many kinds. And most of them do live in a child's world. But some be children with only half of themselves. And as star witness for this statement, I do bring forth Jeff of the Kettles.

For at six summers, Jeff is an old trouper of the Salvation Army. Yea, for the entire space of the lad's life his mother has been a worker in that great organization. And while Jeff's wiry little body resides five hours a day in the schoolroom, his mind doth forever inhabit the street corners where the Salvation Army tripods be.

Last year, saith he, shaking his head like an old man, all the kettles were full of money. Now, only the bottom of any kettle is covered.

Thus it came to pass lately, that Jeff did say at dismissal time, Good-by, Teacher, until the morrow. Then he bethought himself and added, Nay, I'll be seeing thee at the Kettles.

Now such words did perplex me. Verily, I repaired that same day unto the street corners searching for Jeff. And lo, beside a tripod I found him. And he was standing bareheaded in the December winds. His hands were gloveless. And with them he rang his bell continuously. Yet not once did he glance at the holiday-makers. For his eyes were ever upon the contents of his Kettle.

Now Jeff is not the sole owner of shoulders too slight to carry adult burdens. Ever they do stand up like sore thumbs in my schoolroom.

There is Patricia. She owneth much of this world's goods plus a too-beautiful mother. And she saith in a child's direct fashion, I shall buy no lunch at school again. When I ask for her reason she saith, Last night my mother did lose at bridge. The prize was a pink fan made of plumes. And lo, I have seen one in a shop window like unto the one my mother is so cross to lose. And I shall save all of my lunch money and buy it. And as Patricia endeth her story, I see that her little hands are clenched with tenseness.

And long ago there was Tommy. He was the lad who did run across the highway only to be struck down by a truck. And I would that I might forget how he confessed with quick, light breathing, My father hath lost his job, and my mother was weeping when I left for school. And lo, the sound of her crying was still in mine ears. Wherefore I did not look as I crossed the street.

And lo, in those last moments, Tommy did have his ears tipped as if for listening.

Jeff, Patricia, and Tommy. These names are written large in the Book of Over-burdened Children. Yea, they and all their kind be saying in one fashion or another, We'll be seeing thee at the Kettles!

CRYING WATER

Now there came unto me on the first day of school, a distraught young mother. And she held out to me a likely-looking lad of six summers.

And behold, the child clung to her like a leech and whenever she essayed to leave him, he clutched her more tightly and cried in a soft, albeit heartbreaking way.

Then said the mother in desperation, What shall I do?

And I answered, I have somewhat to impart unto thee in the cloakroom. And in the privacy of that darkness I whispered, Take courage, O Mother. This trouble is only for the moment. Always from this goodly number of transplanted little souls, there is one who findeth the uprooting too sudden. Yea, some do tear at themselves and their mothers' skirts. And if they have sufficient temper, some even fall into a heap and kick the floor.

That, admitted the Mother, is hard on the teacher, also.

And I replied, The Teacher goeth to bed that first night with the sounds of a menagerie still in her ears. But behold, I have looked into thy lad's eyes. And if I be not greatly in error, there dwelleth within him a courage of which thou little dreamest.

Then began the Mother to turn to the front her skirt which the child had twisted unto the side seams. And she answered confidently, Perhaps thou knowest the minds of tiny children, and art versed in the hearts of some. But thou understandest not the sensitive nature of my lad. Neither canst thou know the heart of a mother who leaveth her little one to stand, for the first time in his life, alone.

Thou forgettest, said I, that for nine months, and for five hours each day of that time, thy child is mine. Moreover, a part of him belongeth to thirty other little hearts within his classroom. Now, if thou doubtest this, peep through yon door and thou wilt see thirty small lips trembling in sympathy for thy son.

Then said the Mother faintly, If I might wait just beyond the door . . .

Nay, said I. Then would he still hear the rustle of thy skirts. If thou art a wise mother, thou wilt go softly through the outer door. Then will I send thee at the twelfth hour a contented lad. Else am I no part of a teacher.

Now at exactly five minutes after the aforesaid hour, the phone did ring. And I heard the glad sound of the Mother's voice. And she chimed, Verily, thou hast sent me home a man.

And I answered, I would now tell thee of his bravery. After thy departure I saw tears in his eyes. And he did wipe them away hastily, saying, *There is water in mine eyes, but it is not Crying Water.*

Then interrupted the Mother joyously, What thinkest thou he did on the first moment of his return? He straightened his shoulders. Then he gave me the look of a grown man. And he said in a way calculated not to hurt my feelings, I shall have no need of thee tomorrow.

Here Central gave us a warning click. And I went unto my room a flattered woman. Yet not for long.

For suddenly, I was pricked with the remembrance of many useless longings which I still did harbor in mine own heart. Yea, I listened yet for the rustle of their skirts outside the door. And I determined to borrow the courage of my little new lad, and say unto all such outgrown yearnings: I shall have no need of thee tomorrow.

I - C - E

THERE came unto me privily a Schoolteacher. And she was so young that the iridescence was still on her wings. But her eyes were red and swollen. Yea, she told me a long story and the burden of it was Discouragement.

And she said, I explain things an hundred times, but my pupils gaze into space and forget what manner of thing I essayed to teach. I am discomforted and fain would leave the thankless profession. But first, I would know why thou art never disquieted.

And I laughed her to scorn, saying, Alas, I have often thought I cultivated a field which yielded no harvest. And once I sat even as thou sittest. And it was at the beginning of a new term. And I did grieve because the day's reward seemed nothing more than a collection of marbles, pistols, and bubble-gum.

And as I considered these things, a knock sounded upon the door. And straightway there entered the mother of a little lad named Harry. Now Harry had been my pupil of the year before. Hence was I astonished to hear the trembling voice of his mother, saying, I would thou hadst been here when my Harry had to go.

And with a sudden premonition in mine heart I implored, Explain thyself quickly.

And the poor woman said, Harry is dead. And thou wast his teacher. There are things the telling of which might keep mine heart from breaking.

Then she twisted her hands in grief and added, Thou wilt never know what comfort thy spelling lessons had for a dying lad.

Now was I truly astonished. And she spake on, saying, To others it would seem a slight thing. Yet always did my boy esteem it a thing of great worth to be able to spell the word, Ice. Yea, during his last sickness when the fever raced higher, he did crave it continually. Yet not once did he say the word. Instead, he would spell it over and over thus: I-C-E, Mother, please more I-C-E.

Now at these words I did feel a lump within my throat. And I replied, Verily, I have no remembrance of the teaching of such a word.

But the mother contended, Thou didst even more. Thou didst draw on the blackboard a block like unto ice and color it a snowy white. And thou didst inscribe the name thereon. Then did Harry and the other little ones make a game of it, shivering and spelling, I-C-E.

This unburdening of the mother's heart did leave her comforted. And her testimony created for me a memory which shall ever be a sweet and holy joy.

Now when my story was ended, the Young Teacher arose. And her eyes gleamed with unshed tears. And she went her way saying, If ever I be discouraged again, then shall I remember thy little Witness spelling, I-C-E.

MADONNA OF THE OFFICE

THERE was once a shy maiden within my room named Lily. And the title fitted her, for she possessed a fragile, flower-like delicacy. And behold, one morning at the recess period, she came unto me saying happily, The Principal wanteth me in the office.

Now this seemed passing strange, inasmuch as other children usually receive such orders with tears and lamentations. So I watched her trip gayly through the office door. And I saw the Principal shut her within and come down the hallway alone. Therefore spake I unto him with inelegance, saying, I smell a rat. And as he reddened guiltily, I did press mine advantage. Three times, in as many months, said I, thou hast called this child unto thine office. Now, whenever she hears thy footsteps approaching, she gives a little start. If thou dost pass by, she sighs heavily. But if thou callest for her, a look of delight shineth on her face. Tell me, dost thou trot her on thy knees, or feed her lollipops?

This is no joking matter, said the Principal gravely. It is a situation requiring much silence and tact. However, I must needs get some reports from mine office. If thou wilt pass by at that moment, I will leave the door slightly ajar. Then mayest thou become a confederate in this mystery.

Now I hastened to obey these commands. And I looked through the narrow opening. And, behold, at first my gaze went beyond the windows. And I saw bare branches black against the wintry sky, and unmelted snow in tree crotches. Then beheld I the office with its bleak-looking bookcases and desk. But within the Principal's swivel chair was a scene of domesticity. Yea, a strange woman sat there and Lily lay within her arms in utter contentment. Moreover, in a quick flash, I beheld the woman also. And, lo, she resembled no lily. She was clad in much-bedraggled finery. Likewise, her hair was anointed with peroxide and flaunted a rakish red beret. But real emotion trembled on her painted lips; and above all the cheapness, the look of mother-love was a-bloom on her face. Thus sat the two, as in a dream, saying nothing. Neither was there any sound save the ticking of the office clock. And no movement save that of the child's arm reaching up to the woman's neck.

Then as suddenly as the tableau had begun, it ended. The Principal came out and closed the door.

It's the mother, began I in an excited whisper. But wherefore was she never mentioned in my visit to the grandparents?

There hath been an ugly scandal, said the Principal. And the Law hath given the child unto the father. Moreover, he hath made many dangerous threats concerning what he will do if ever there should occur a meeting betwixt these two. For this reason I confided not in any soul. For if there be trouble, it must be on mine own head. Now the Principal has the soul of a poet.

Wherefore he ended, I can see no harm in giving two Displaced Persons a few moments together. Verily, it doth gladden me to see them beyond all awareness of a school office or bill of divorcement.

Then, even as he spake, the recess period ended, and I hastened unto my children. And lo, as we passed the closed office, the Principal was pacing up and down reading the morning paper.

Still walking post? asked I in a low voice. Nay, he answered, I have greater business: I am guarding the sanctity of a Home.

LOUELLA

Every Teacher hath kidded herself into believing that bracelets and bananas do walk. Yet there always cometh the day when she has to admit that the legs do belong to an Artful Dodger. Which being interpreted meaneth a thief.

Now were it not for the quivering lips of the lad whose lunch is taken, or the sobbing of the maiden bereft of a bracelet, no teacher would face the truth. For it is a grievous thing to look into a sea of fresh young faces and know that one of them is spying out the land for another hold-up.

Yet such illicit business did lately flourish within my room. And the hands of the thief were deft, and the feet thereof like unto hinds' feet for swiftness. And it was ever the most cherished perfume bottle that was gone. Yea, and the reddest-cheeked apple, or the cookie with the pink frosting.

And it seemed that never would I discover my little Sleight-of-Hand Artist. Then suddenly one day a long-lost bow of red hair ribbon did rise in bright shame above a certain damsel's bosom. And, lo, the guilty bosom did belong unto Louella, the oldest pupil in my room.

Now Louella did hail from the back-wash of the town. And she wore a daring, inscrutable expression. Verily, her hard little eyes were of metallic brightness like unto shiny black chinquapins.

And at her guilt my soul was indeed vexed within me. For she did continue to reap where she had not sown, and gather where she had not strawed.

Then came the Day of the Losing of the Rubber Stamps. Now the stamps were the property of the school. Likewise, every lad and damsel lived ever in the hope of seeing magic impressions stamped upon some worth-while paper.

And I spake unto my pupils concerning this last act of plunder. And Louella showed no guilt or shame. Then stepped I to the back of the room where all the contents of the tables were exposed. And lo, within Louella's table saw I the forty and five missing stamps. Wherefore said I with great urgency, Let everyone bring forth whatever is within his or her table.

Now these words were a dark saying unto Louella. For she did thrust in her crafty little hands and brought forth nothing. Then said I again, Feel within thy tables a second time.

Now I know not what I expected. But of a surety it was not what I received. For Louella did bring forth every rubber stamp. And she looked at me boldly and said with well-feigned astonishment, Lord, G——, Almighty.

Now such large profanity from such small lips did give all of us gooseflesh. Even I, her teacher, did feel constrained to shout in the manner of an alley tough, Stick 'em up. Yet I held my peace. For something deep within me said, Perhaps the remedy for Louella lieth under thine own roof.

For I remembered how easy it always was for Louella to take. And I wondered if perchance she might find it hard to receive. And if, indeed, she had any armor against Love.

Therefore I did take her aside privily. And Louella said rudely, What dost thou want?

And I replied, I want nothing. But whenever thou wantest that which is not thine own, if thou wilt come to me, lo, I will buy it for thee. Yea, even unto the half of my salary.

And she said with a strange look of satisfaction, Okay.

Now this was a dangerous psychology, and one calculated to deplete a teacher's purse. But this much I know: That I have bought naught for Louella, and that whereas once she stole, she now stealeth no more.

MISSY-GIRL

$\mathcal{A}$T the end of a school day when all the other little lads and damsels had departed, there lingered a downcast sorrowful little fellow. And he held out a tiny scrap of paper with the name, David Fairby, inscribed thereon.

Now as I wondered over the meaning of the inscription, the lad said in a low shamed voice, My father hath gotten what he calleth a divorce from me and my mother. And she hath sent unto thee this new name which I must wear.

And I said, I like the new name called Fairby. To me it hath a lovely, sunny sound. Yea, it reminds me of a bright blue day.

It was once my mother's name, confided the lad. But never before hath it belonged to me.

And I said, Wouldst thou be greatly surprised to know that thy teacher did once lose her name also?

Then the dark pain did leave the lad's eyes and he said simply, Tell me.

And I said, I was three times thine age, and nineteen is full young for a teacher. Now as I did enter my schoolyard for the first time all the children stood at the doorway to bid me welcome. And as they perceived that I half-skipped and half-ran in mine eagerness to reach them, then did one little maiden cry happily to the others, Yonder cometh our Missy-Girl. And from that day onward, my pupils did always call me by that lovely name. Yea, even until I went to make my habitation at a faraway school.

And why, questioned the lad of the new name, did not those children of another school call thee Missy-Girl?

And I did confess, These new children could understand the *Missy* part of my name. But never saw they any further need of the part called *Girl*.

Then declared David, I like best the name thou now wearest. For it is longer and harder to say.

And then felt I a little chin on my shoulder in new companionship. And a small voice did entreat, When thou tellest the class of my new name, wilt thou also tell them that thou once hadst to change thine own?

And I answered, Yea.

Now that night I asked God to lighten the burden of the lad who must always wear his mother's maiden name. And I added vaingloriously:

And when thou comest to chose my Celestial Title, O Lord, wilt thou look with favor on the name *Missy-Girl?*

THE RETURN

Be not deceived if some Doubter saith that an eighteen-year-old War Veteran hath no place within these pages. For verily several have crossed the school threshold since their return from far countries. And save for the stature and a certain grave look in their eyes, they might still be tiny lads arriving for another day at school.

Such an one is Phillip. And he came unto me during a recess hour. And of this I was glad. For children be frank creatures. And Phillip had lost his right arm.

Now he had entered with much gaiety. And he talked much of nothing. For his words were hollow, empty things used for the purpose of concealing his loss.

And I replied in like fashion. And when I saw his long legs reaching beyond his old table where he had seated himself, I said foolishly, Who would have thought that such a tiny tyke as thou wouldst grow such long roots? Yet all the time was I lamenting because Phillip had builded a wall between himself and all his old world.

And straightway I determined to break down the wall. Wherefore said I guardedly, Hast thou seen thy best girl Laurie?

And he answered, Nay. And he added with a fine show of unconcern, I can take all that has been handed out to me. That is, all save Laurie's pity.

And I rejoiced at his words. For now did I know that the wall was beginning to crumble. And I laughed him to scorn, saying, Who would have believed that one who swung so reckless a rifle, could now turn into a deserter?

And he laughed bitterly and said, She shall never have the chance to tell me that our romance hath wilted around the edges.

And he tapped his artificial arm until it gave forth a strange metallic ring. And he laughed again and said, Even thou canst hardly expect her to show any keenness for this.

And I replied, I have not forgotten that Laurie was thy faithful shadow throughout thy school years. Yea, I am persuaded that she will never love thee less because thou didst give the best part of thyself, even thy right arm, for thy Country.

And Phillip said, Thy words sound swell. But things just don't link up that easily.

Then confessed I, and withheld nothing. And I said, Laurie and I have had a long conversation concerning thee. And I watched what was happening in her eyes. And lo, all is well.

Now did Phillip turn white, and he said with desperate urgency, Always thou hast understood me. What wouldst thou have me to do?

And I said, Take off thy rag-tag suit of a civilian. And get thee hence quickly and put on thy uniform. Yea, and all thy decorations, even unto the Croix de Guerre.

And Phillip looked at me as at a wild woman. And he said, I will not go to her arrayed as one of Lady Astor's horses.

But I contended, She is a woman, and I have looked deep into her eyes.

Then Phillip sware a great oath and he said, By Jiminy, I will go as I am; and there can be no harm in seeing her.

And I hid all feelings of sympathy, and I smote him on the bad arm, saying, Hasten, before I get my old paddle.

And he arose and went out smiling.

Now the moment he was gone, I was smitten with a hurtful memory. Yea, it came back in a flood. For I recollected how soft and trusting had been Phillip's little hand when I guided it in the intricate making of his A B C's. And I laid mine head down upon his table and wept.

ASHES TO ASHES

Now there came unto me during a number lesson, Mikal, our Eternal Questioner. And her little polka-dotted dress did rustle with inquiry.

Thou sayest, she affirmed, that if I have *one* thing and take *nothing* from it that I do still have *one*. I have not found it so. For I did bury one dead Kitty in the ground. And behold, when I went to dig it up again, there was nothing left.

Now after hearing this strange new number fact, I said within myself, Here is a chance to speak somewhat of the Immortality of the Soul. And I said, Thy Kitty is still there. But it hath changed unto dust. So do the bodies of persons also. But their souls return to God.

Then did Mikal lift wondering eyes upon every creature in the room. And I knew she was sampling with particular savour the thought of Ashes to Ashes, and Dust to Dust.

Now it fell out an hour later as Mikal cleaned the shelves and ledges of the room, that she paused before a window sill. Yea, she did gaze long and searchingly upon it. And lifting puzzled eyes, she said with deep awe and gravity, *Whose dust is this?*

Then did I glance around that room and think on the many things which had invested it with life.

Yea, I re-lived the glow and sparkle of it all: the bright-hued skirts and gay ribbons, the golden curls behind rosy ears, and the gleam of baby rings still on schoolboy fingers.

And I spake unto myself and I said, The vagaries of thirty little growing souls are enough to cause the dry bones of any teacher to be revived. Surely, therefore, when one of the profession turns to dust, it is stardust.

And I prayed that no unfeeling person might ever ask concerning the ashes of any teacher: *Whose dust is this?*

THE KISS

Not many years past, there was a time of War. And Roberta's father belonged unto the Navy of these United States. And lo, he fought for three years on many seas. Yet always did he bring Roberta to school as he began a new mission for his Uncle Sam.

Thus it fell out one snowy morning that he rode the little damsel into the schoolhouse piggy-back fashion. And the twain did make a pretty picture: The tall man with gleaming stars and braid, and Roberta with her yellow curls floating out over his shoulder.

And while he lowered her slowly in his arms he said, Daddy hath a cold today. Wherefore he cannot kiss his Honey Bee upon the mouth.

And he touched lightly with his lips that spot on Roberta's cheek where the dimple is wont to come and go.

Now when he was departed, Roberta reached up swiftly to the place where he had mislaid the kiss. And straightway she did perform a miracle. Yea, she caught that intangible caress between her determined little thumb and forefinger. Then with a pretty air of triumph she did place it squarely upon her mouth.

LET JOY BE UNCONFINED

*Y*EARS ago, during a tornado, there did sing and dance within my schoolroom a tiny Crown Prince of Comedy. But that lad now sleepeth on Anzio Beachhead. And often have I said within myself that for sheer nonsense and bravery, I should never see his like again.

Then suddenly on a Post-war morning there sounded a bold knock on my door. And lo, a second Star Comedian stood upon the threshold.

And his name was Timothy. And he came prancing in with feet turned outward after the manner of Clowns. Likewise did his bush of sandy hair stand in tufts like unto a Jester's. And his six-year-old mouth tilted upwards in perpetual merriment.

Moreover, he took no seat, but squatting on his wiry haunches, proceeded to fold up, joint by joint, like a jackknife.

And instantly there sounded a pleased tongue-clicking amongst his observers. Yea, from that moment Timothy had a reputation to maintain. And I, his Teacher, did have a daily prayer session that I might deal aright with the thirty Souls anointed daily with Timothy's Oil of Gladness.

Now the lad's favorite seat was hard by my side. And he delighted in patting mine arm. And at the same time would he blow his breath up mine open sleeve until it resembled an inflated balloon. And I winced as I accepted his ministrations. Albeit, what provoked and proved me far more, was the knowledge that his pats and wet kisses were filching vital work from himself and his classmates.

These were the several manners of his behavior: to wit, interrupting an important lesson by holding his ear far out from his head. Then apparently sawing off the offending member with his pencil.

However, if this method brought not the desired acclamation, then would he distend his small stomach to the length of a span, at the same time testing the humor of his audience by placing bits of mashed potatoes within the wells of his dimples.

But perchance, if he still felt cheated of his clown's applause, then proved he me further by drawing white polka-dots on his shoes and those of his fellows. Likewise, on Spring days he pasted petals of red roses on his ten fingers in imitation of the violently colored nails of some women.

And so it came to pass, after many days of too much Timothy, that I besought him earnestly, saying, Take off all foolish adornment. Then perchance thou wilt get a taste for thy lessons. And the little Rowdy answered jauntily, I tried lessons but they are too strong!

Now all such tributaries did feed the stream of my impatience. And I resorted unto all manner of punishment save those of the Hand. And lo, as I sought for a Newer Method, I discovered the loss of mine eyeglasses. And simultaneously my glance did fall upon a toy elephant which the children had fashioned from an huge potato. And behold, the elephant was scrutinizing the world through my spectacles. Moreover, this difficult feat had been accomplished by bending the sidepieces of the glasses past repair.

Then indeed did mine indignation wax unto hot action. And using the Hand Method, I put four and two sharp spanks on the rear of Timothy's trousers.

And lo, after the space of five minutes, the little culprit sidled up to me. And with no resentment saith in ardent avowal, Thou art still my Sweetheart.

Here was something beyond calculation: that a teacher at such a moment receive sincere approbation. Wherefore went I unto Timothy's abode. And there his grandsire told me that the lad's mother had remarried, leaving behind her five children. And he added, Timothy hath possessed the comical ways of a clown since his birth. And he doth ever display this gift at school to gain your attention. For he hopes thereby to win your affection. For Timothy is hungry for love.

Now this knowledge did unsteady me. But I hardened mine heart for the lad's good and that of his classmates. And I commanded him to withdraw himself. And for the space of three days he moved not unto my side but sat afar off. And the Spirit of Nonsense seemed clean departed from him.

Then upon a certain day as he marched out for recess caught I the old dare in his eyes. Yet realized I not the grave import of his tactics until a small Informant did point to a near-by culvert, shrilling, Timothy hath climbed far up into the big terra cotta and lo, he cannot budge himself one way or the other.

Then I called frantically unto the Janitor. And I urged him in my distress and ignorance to burst the pipe with an axe lest the lad suffocate.

71 }

But the ancient Ethiopian went empty-handed unto the dark opening. And he used the calm yet wheedling tones of his race, saying, Easy, Son. Git down from them knees and flatten down. Then spread-eagle out backwards.

Now it was eight agonizing minutes before Timothy, pale and crumpled, stood before me. And he followed me silently into the schoolroom, gazing with routine hopefulness at the empty chair on my right. And lo, two large gritty tears had usurped the place of the potatoes in his dimples. And he performed no shenanigans, but pressed his wet nose against my shoulder, saying, I am cold.

And behold, I steeled myself, answering, Thou wilt soon be warm.

But Timothy contended further, saying, Yea, but I am cold *inside*.

Then melted I somewhat, saying, Thou mayest sit beside me.

And instantly the lad's eyes were starry promises as he saith, All that thou askest of me hereafter, that will I do. And he leaned forward gazing with longing upon my frilled sleeve.

Now meant I to say, Timothy, I've a mind to take you unto the Spanking Tree. But suddenly mine heart went back unto mine other Lad who would nevermore charm away the world's weariness by his drollery and nonsense. And I reasoned further, What harm can there be in filling a little hungry heart by so simple a measure as blowing upon an arm?

Wherefore, I did forget the exact words of my rebuke. And I spake thusly: Timothy, I've a mind to let you just once more make a balloon of my sleeve.

And Timothy, with silt deposits forming where his teardrops had been, did consent.

THE TOP-LOFTY LADY

T came to pass on a day nigh unto the Christmas season, that a knock of authority did sound upon our classroom door. And thirty pairs of eyes fastened themselves upon the knob with the old amaze and expectancy. Yet no Kris Kringle did jingle in. But a Top-Lofty Lady with plumes and pearls made a sweeping entrance. Yea, she was clad in such fine raiment that the children gazed upon her as at a showy window dressing.

Now this woman owned many stocks and bonds, and had great power and pull. Verily, her works were continually praising her in the newspapers as well as within the gates.

And she gushed forth effusively, What dear, dear Little Ones! How intelligent and how pretty! And as she spoke her voice was sweet like unto the playing of an Aeolian Harp. But her eyes were like unto cold sapphires. And her double chin was the Chin of Pride.

And she continued virtuously, I have brought some Christmas baskets from our Club. For lo, we were told that thou hast two or three Little Ones in dire need.

Then did she gaze past the heads of the sheltered and well-loved. And her eyes rested on a veritable ragamuffin of a maiden.

Yea, the little damsel was clothed in faded red percale. And dingy wisps of hair did almost conceal her intelligent blue eyes.

And straightway the Lady said with no lowering of her voice, It never faileth that those who save no money for their Children's Santa Claus, likewise have no water or soap for baths. Then did she call in a voice of authority, John. And lo, there appeared in the doorway, an Ethiopian Chauffeur bearing two Yuletide baskets.

And forthwith a strange thing happened: The faces of my children which so shortly before had glowed with the wonder of Christmas-tide, now looked at the woman with eyes that weighed and were exceedingly guarded. For it takes children to put grown-ups into their proper classification. And verily, my damsel of the red percale dress had seen clearest of them all. Yea, she had perceived a thin veneer which could crack and scratch.

Furthermore at our worship period the next morning she did utter this revealing prayer: O God, bless the fine Lady with the two chins, and make her a Christian.

TOMORNING

*T*HIS day hath been too tumultuous to hold. Outside, blossoms have shattered and clouds tumbled. Within the windy doorway I stood at school's end, as battered as the universe. Around me swirled the First Grade, chattering, pushing, nipping one another. As the last curls and cowlicks tossed from sight, their owners lifted up their voices with one accord, crying, Good-by, Teacher.

Then, just as I sank down, becalmed, I deemed, at last, there was a sharp prod on my toe. And gazing downward I beheld Rosie, Creator of Subtle Phrases. She was describing an arc of impatience around me, calling blithely, I fain would say more than Good-by. And she paused a moment touching the ruffles of my pink skirt. Then she lifted her eyes to the silvery sheen of the cherry tree beyond the window. And she added with a little catch of pleasure in her voice, I would say, I'll be seeing thee Tomorning.

Here was a new word for a new day. Involuntarily, I straightened my tired shoulders and mussed hair. And instead of starting homeward, I found myself gazing at the lace of the cherry tree, and pondering over this last deft word of Rosie's coinage.

Tomorning, I mused, must sparkle somewhere between the

last morning star and the grown-up world called tomorrow. For verily, as Rosie hath pronounced it with tinkles of musical laughter, it doth suggest dawn at its youngest: Some fleeting, iridescent time much lighter and finer-spun than an ordinary day.

And forthwith I sighed as I arose to pack mine equipment. For I was remembering with nostalgia that all adults were once heirs to Rosie's captivating Realm of Tomorning. Yea, and I wondered as I journeyed homeward, just when one passeth the borderland of childhood and findeth its magic departed: those days of elation over a silver-sprinkled Valentine or tinsel-winged angel. Childish beliefs in simple ceremonies like unto wishing on a star, or bowing to the new moon. Yea, and faith in Santa Claus. And unquestioning trust in all mankind. . . .

Then suddenly, I quickened my pace remembering a tryst to keep. For well I know that on the morrow Rosie and her kind will stand around me in an eager, expectant circle. And try as I may to step within their magical world, I shall be alien. For children are the sole owners of Tomorning. Yea, and lately they have acquired another possession: a suspicious, untidy world to refashion.

At the thought of this last task, I gazed backward once more to the cherry tree for reassurance. And lo, I beheld it shimmering with the magic of Eternal Spring. And mine heart did quicken. For then knew I that as long as petals do uncurl, or faith sings in the hearts of Little Ones, none of us need fear today's grievous propaganda or its long-range predictions. Because the Rosies of this world can always give back unto us a Tomorning patterned straight from the heart of a Child.

If ye doubt this, then gaze unseen at any group of innocent Little Ones: Tomorning's dawn is written on their faces.

{ 76